Dedication

Dedicated to my godchild Nico and my dear godfather Nikos, whose love for the sea was truly inspiring.

About the author

Born and raised in London, this author has spent considerable time traversing the Mediterranean, calling Cyprus, Spain, and Greece his other homes. With a creative streak that has been nurtured for over 15 years, his passion lies in illustration and the art of storytelling, where he skillfully captivates the imagination. His latest endeavor, a children's book series, is a heartfelt attempt to preserve the rich tapestry of Greek traditions. Through his vivid illustrations and engaging narratives, he aims to keep these cultural treasures alive for future generations, safeguarding them from the brink of oblivion. This dedication not only showcases his artistic talents but also his commitment to cultural preservation, making his work an invaluable bridge between past and future.

© 2024 Captain Kitty Niki and Fisherman Nikos
- Written and illustrated by Demitri Karayianni

On the beautiful Greek Island,
Spetses in the Hellenic Sea,
Where the sun loves to play
and life's spirit is free.

Lived a humble fisherman, Nikos by name,
Whose life's destined course was fishing,
It was his claim to fame.

Passed down from his father
and forefathers of yore,
the sea was his calling, the
tales of the shore.

Despite Spetses' waters, he'd traverse,
He was known as the fisherman under a curse.

Years spent casting his nets, a struggle, no less, His catch was always meager, causing him distress.

One morning, on his route to port, Nikos saw movement in the back of his tricycle truck,

There, under his nets, he found a little kitten
helplessy stuck

Trembling and weak, in need of aid,
Her fate and his, were about to be made.

Little did Nikos know what was about to unfold,
His cat was given the name 'Niki' after the goddess of victory,

Like her, she grew so strong and so bold.

One sunny morning, Nikos was on his way to the old port, while Kitty Niki stood on his roof as his escort.

They arrived on board Nikos' fishing boat, all gleaming white,

and set off across the turquoise waters of Spetses with all their might.

Nikos set course for his usual fishing spot,
and prepared his fishing nets to plot.

Nikos at the helm, steering port and starboard, while
Kitty Niki stood at the bow, on watch and all startled.

She swung her paws to the starboard side and meowed very loudly. Nikos, surprised by the movement, cast his nets so proudly.

He reeled in his nets, filled with fish;
that's the best catch yet, just as he wished.

Kitty Niki and Fisherman Nikos jumped for joy,
the boat rocking left and right,
while Nikos the fisherman shouted,
'Ahoy!

Nikos looked after the kitten,
feeding her lots of fish.
As days turned into weeks,
she grew to fully flourish.

The locals spoke proudly of Nikos the Fisherman and his hero, Kitty Niki, as the island fish market flourished with plentiful fish very quickly.

Day after day, they caught away,
with no curse in sight.
Kitty Niki, no longer a stray, is here to
stay with no fright.

They dined every night, inviting
guests and friends,
with plenty of food and dancing,
setting the island's trend.

The islanders praised Nikos and Kitty Niki
for their success,
legends of the island Spetses
and nothing less.

Nikos the Fisherman finally had his claim to fame, and rejoiced with his cat, Captain Kitty Niki, who did the same.

Grateful for the life of abundance they lived in Greece,

catching fish every day,
A life full in every single way.

THE END

© 2024 Captain Kitty Niki and Fisherman Nikos
- Written and illustrated by Demitri Karayianni

Printed in Great Britain
by Amazon